My Truth 180°

360° is Not An Option

Howishia McFadden

ZCP

My Truth 180°: 360° is Not An Option

Copyright © 2024 by Howishia McFadden

INSPIRATIONAL SPEAKER | MENTOR | ENTREPRENEUR
McFadden Associates
www.howishiamcfadden.com
howishiamcfadden@gmail.com
Social Media: @howishiamcfadden

ZCP

Zyia Christian Publishing, LLC
drdavis@thebookbirthingmidwife.com

Unless otherwise noted, all Scripture quotations are taken from the blueletterbible.org

Front Cover Design: BrandingLosAngeles.com / Kwon Hogan

Back Cover Design: Zyia Christian Publishing, LLC

Photographer: Muhammad White

Interior Text Design: Zyia Christian Publishing, LLC

Distributed by IngramSpark.

ISBN: 979-8-218-41673-7

Dedication

This book is dedicated to everyone who struggles but continues to get up every day for everyone else and make it happen.

Table of Content

CHAPTER 1: Somewhere Around 360° — 1

CHAPTER 2: It Had To Happen — 5

CHAPTER 3: It Had To Happen, Continued... — 11

CHAPTER 4: The Kept Secret Exposed — 13

CHAPTER 5: The Journal Speaks — 15

CHAPTER 6: Now Whattt? — 20

CHAPTER 7: Stand Up For Something — 21

CHAPTER 8: Confessions — 23

CHAPTER 9: The Reddest of All Red Flags — 26

CHAPTER 10: Trust Me, He Hasn't Forgotten — 30

CHAPTER 11: Plea Deal... — 32

CHAPTER 12: Reverse Needed to Escalate — 35

CHAPTER 13: Red Flags - Bloody Flags — 37

CHAPTER 14: The Encounter — 40

CHAPTER 15: Then Comes Baby — 43

CHAPTER 16: The Kicker ... 47

CHAPTER 17: Test Designed Testimony ... 51

CHAPTER 18: Better Than Better ... 53

CHAPTER 19: Facing Reality ... 54

CHAPTER 20: Give Us This Day ... 56

CHAPTER 21: Momma's Baby ... 59

CHAPTER 22: Forgive & Release ... 61

CHAPTER 23: What Can I Surrender ... 64

CHAPTER 24: My Truth Pointers 360... 240... 180 ... 66

GRATEFUL IS ME ... 69

MY DAILY AFFIRMATIONS ... 72

CHAPTER ONE

Somewhere Around 360°

A few years ago, I struggled to live a full life. I was merely surviving mentally; the best way I knew how was by putting the best on the outside. One day, life handed me an unexpected twist. I was embarking on my first-ever Women's Prayer Retreat. The women in attendance came from all walks of life. It was one of the most personal encounters with the Most High I had ever experienced. I recommend that everyone experience a prayer retreat, whether for a day, a weekend, or a week. It will change your life for the better. The eye-opening, soul-searching experience will reveal your powerful emotions and characteristics you didn't know existed.

While at the retreat, I called home to check on the kids. While speaking with my daughter, Angel, I told

1

her she had braided my hair too tightly and would have to take it out immediately when I got home. We joked about it, and suddenly, she began to cry. My heart sank into my stomach. "What's wrong?" I asked. The silence on the other end was deafening. "Nothing," she finally replied. But, that was far from the truth because, at a young age, she had never cried for anything.

A voice spoke to me and advised me to tell Angel to take the time and write a letter to me, her dad, and her siblings to address what bothered her. During the retreat, I learned to be truthful with myself before I could reveal the truth to anyone else. I asked her to do me a favor, to be truthful with her words. Even if it hurts, it must be done. Trust me when I say that this was a Godly move.

Upon arriving home, I was excited and happy to see everyone. As soon as I arrived and entered the house, I called Angel into my room and asked her, "Did you do what I asked concerning the letters?" "Oh, Mom," she said, trying to make light of the situation. I could tell she was holding back. "Did you do it?" I asked more firmly. "Yes, I did," she replied, but she didn't move a muscle. "Where is it?" I asked. Angel finally handed me the letter with hesitation.

As I intently studied each word, never in my wildest dreams did I think I would be reading the content of her letter. No one prepared me for my daughter's expression of being filled with such anger toward life in the first few lines. Later in the letter, I learned the reason behind the despair.

I realized that God sent me to the retreat to prepare me for what my family and I were about to endure. I thanked God for guiding us to this point. The truth had to come out.

In the letter, my daughter explained that at the age of twelve, she was molested by their former babysitter's brother. She was terrified to talk about it, and it was killing her slowly. She hated me for allowing them to do this to her. While I read her words of truth, I tried my hardest to keep my composure without showing any facial expressions. In my head, I imagined running out, grabbing my heat (gun), and ending that man's life. It was a drastic, impulsive reaction. But, what would your response be if your child told you they were being or have been molested, especially by the people you trusted with their being? If it wasn't for the prayer retreat, I would have been writing my truth from a jail cell.

Often, children never speak up because adults downplay the situation or sweep it under the rug. I refused to act that way. This needed to be addressed, or else no good would come of my daughter's life.

Not once did I question Angel to give her the impression that she did something to provoke his actions. She is an innocent child with good values. My mind wandered back to years earlier when she became a child who liked to be alone. All the pieces started falling into place.

Parents, soon-to-be parents, and guardians, any adults. Period. When you notice a child's change in behavior, seek to understand the cause.

I believe, as guardians, we have given our children too much lead on privacy until we have become blind. So much is happening in the world, and I will not allow my kids to feel like they can have locked doors. Why? Because they don't pay bills. When you are grown and pay your bills, you can lock all the doors in your house. I am here to protect, not to please.

CHAPTER TWO

It Had to Happen

My first rational reaction was to embrace Angel and tell her, "We will get through this together." My mind raced with questions, and my heart was beating rapidly. When I looked at her face and said those words, I saw her relief. Her expression said, *Wow, I don't have to carry this burden like a ton of bricks weighing me down anymore.* I would never forget that look. However, my day was far from over.

Later that evening, I was in the kitchen washing dishes. I called my youngest daughter, Delilah, to chat. While we had a light conversation, I reiterated that if anyone were to touch her in a way that wasn't right she should tell me. "Yes, Mom. How many times have you told us that?" "I'm serious," I replied with assertiveness. Sensing my non-joking tone, she said, "Yes, Mom, I know. Why are you asking me about this?"

I didn't want to tell her all the details, but looking into her eyes I knew I couldn't lie. I stood at the kitchen sink and said, "Delilah, something bad happened, and you need to know about it." She barely finished asking what happened before I broke down into tears. Through my sobbing, I tried to remain strong. I told her that Angel had been molested. Delilah cried, asking who did this to her. She repeatedly asked me who it was, but I couldn't bear to speak his name. I asked her to assure me that she would tell me if anything ever happened to her.

She kept asking for his name. I mustered up the courage to utter the name, *Paul*. The way my child yelped at his name made my skin crawl. She kept whispering, "Seven years ago, seven years ago." I asked her what had happened, feeling a rage bubble in my veins. Tears streamed down her face, and she nearly choked on her words. She told me that seven years ago, the same man had touched her. He told her to like it, because the other girls did. The wet plate I held slipped from my fingers and shattered on the floor.

I couldn't believe what I was hearing. I froze with shock. It was only going to get worse from there. Worse than I could have ever have imagined. When my baby girl told me this, she was eleven. Seven years ago meant she would have been... four years old. What kind of monster does this to children?

Delilah said she thought it was normal, and he bought her anything she wanted, like happy meals, candy, and toys. He would touch her leg and other areas, asking if she liked it. Delilah started naming the other girls he told her about. As she spoke, I could see the awakening in her eyes. The memories of the darkest places in her past were emerging to the surface. She looked at me with cold eyes, then told me to talk to my son, Dexter.

Instinctively, I went to my room and started loading my piece. A peaceful resolution was the farthest thing from my mind. Sitting on my bed with the 9 mm in my lap, I breathed slowly to try and calm down. Delilah sat next to me. I asked what she meant when she said ask DEXTER.

She called Dexter to come from his room. There was no response, so I yelled for him. Soon, he came into my room. Delilah started yelling at him, saying, "Tell Momma what happened to you! It's okay! Tell Mom what Paul did! She knows the truth." I stared at my children. My daughter was wild and frantic, and my son solemn and quiet. They held this in for years, expertly keeping each other's secrets. I calmly asked Dexter what happened, hugging Delilah to my chest. Dexter told me that Paul beat him and made him perform a sexual act on him.

I want to keep this story PG, but these details are not a joke. My heart shattered. Not only one child, not two, but all three of them have been suffering for the majority of their lives.

At that moment, I felt like a failed mother. I thought I worked hard enough to provide financially and offer love and attention to my family. But, I couldn't protect them from this monster. This man portrayed the role of sainthood to deceive everyone. Don't get me started on the pedophiles that attend church every Sunday, waiting for a target with candy or a hug. As parents, we may think that because they go to church, they are good. That is a lie.

Back to my son, if I hadn't known God before that day, it would've been the end of that man's life. All I could see was blood. I had countless unanswered questions about who knew, what happened, where, when, and why.

I rushed to the kitchen and called out to Angel. She didn't have a clue what I was about to say. I told her that she wasn't alone. The same man had assaulted her brother and sister. As a family, we stood in the kitchen, sobbing and embracing each other.

The details of that day will never escape my mind. When I composed myself, I consoled them and told them to write down everything they had remembered. No other experience could have prepared me for that horror. Can you imagine trying not to cry or react out of anger while being strong for your children? How hard that must be? I was their protector, and I wanted to take them away to a place where they would never be found by predators and never return to reality.

I started questioning my abilities as a mother. Was I a workaholic? Did I not pay attention? Was there a distraction in my life, a boo thing, or what? I could only control so much about the people my kids were influenced by and who surrounded them. I wasn't out partying in the streets when I hired a babysitter. I trusted these people almost like family. I thought they were good. But, that night was the longest night of my life. I couldn't sleep. I called my boss and informed her I had a family emergency and wouldn't be in the next day. I was running on an adrenaline high; no drugs or Red Bull was needed.

After a restless night with a heavy heart, I pulled myself together and went to the police station with the kids to file a police report. I have respect for law enforcement, but if I could have taken justice into my own hands, I never would have gone to them.

I won't pretend that I didn't have doubts about their abilities. I wanted to put all the predators six feet underground—no time in jail or wasting taxpayers' dollars. I'm keeping it real. It may sound harsh, but I pray that nothing like this ever happens to you or anyone you encounter. You will never understand the severity and effects it has on a person until you've lived through it yourself.

The detectives took Angel into an interrogation room first, then the other kids followed. Their statements, recounting what happened in their own words, were videotaped. It felt like they were in the interrogation room for an eternity. The detective escorted Dexter out, shaking his head in disgust. He told a fellow officer he needed a break and couldn't imagine this happening to his children.

Several times, I questioned why I stepped foot into the precinct. The voice of God reminded me that I came here to handle it the right way with *no blood on my hands*. The detectives explained the next steps of the investigation, stating it wouldn't resolve overnight, but justice would be served. The process was long and excruciating, but it had to be done. It drained my family's energy. We were emotionally, mentally, and physically worn out. Before all of this, I never had to take so many medications in my life.

CHAPTER THREE

It Had to Happen, Continued...

Here we go... After a month-and-a-half-long investigation, the detectives contacted Paul and brought him into custody. Initially, he denied everything, of course. He knew he was caught and backed into a corner. After he was questioned and released, word started spreading like a virus, and I began my investigation.

I had just finished my Crime Scene Investigation (CSI) classes and there was no way I wouldn't put my knowledge and schooling to good use. If someone had been murdered, the cops would have made that their priority. But, for this situation, I had to put in the work. I couldn't stand aside and wait.

One day, I received a call from a family member of Paul's saying that they heard what happened. The cops came to their house, and they explained what they knew. People are funny, aren't they? They started sharing the truth about Paul messing with kids years ago. Yet, they kept quiet when they needed to speak up the most. They were afraid to speak, afraid to admit that they were allowing a monster near their children. Not this chick! I refused to be the one who swept the issue under the rug. I wouldn't ignore what happened.

CHAPTER FOUR

The Kept Secret Exposed

Fast Forward – The officers finally arrested him for the charges of first- and third-degree child sexual assault. They didn't consider my baby girl Delilah a victim because they felt there wasn't "enough" physical contact. Like, really, what is enough? That was something serious. You get what I'm saying! Is this really the system that I'm supposed to believe in? Where was the justice for my precious Delilah and the other kids out there?

I attended every hearing and bond reduction. My employment came third for once in my life. God planned to put that job in my path, and I was willing to lose it if it came down to that. This was a mandatory sacrifice that had to be made for my children and so many others. I definitely couldn't let them down after they displayed the strength to confide in me. It was bad enough that I failed them by allowing this to happen.

Some adults have thanked me for staying on top of the case. Others have expressed that when they were younger, they were molested and forced to keep quiet. I remember a young lady saying, "Thank you for being my voice because my own mother wouldn't believe that her boyfriend molested me." Her mother told her not to say anything because he would leave and the bills wouldn't get paid. How could a mom sacrifice her child to keep a man? Could you imagine making that choice? It happens more often than you think.

Then, an older lady expressed to me how her pastor's son repeatedly raped her. He later impregnated her, and they moved her away. In this day and age, you have to be more careful...

CHAPTER FIVE

The Journal Speaks

~ SILENT NO MORE ~

Insert from Angel's Journal:

As a child, I was always happy, enjoyed doing fun things and making friends. I never bothered anyone. At times, I often stayed to myself. A child that never spoke, because I cared about everyone else's feelings but mine. But, I knew that many people cared about me and loved me until a piece of me was taken away. The older I got, the more this part of my life destroyed me so much because I felt empty. Sometimes, I wondered why I'm still here. Why me? Did I have to be the young girl that would live in fear of men all her life and not trust people anymore? I was so pure and innocent. I was young, and I was a child. I never bothered anybody. I always had a smile on my face and now that jolly little girl inside of me will never be the same. At the age of twelve, my life was OVER!

From that time, I looked at everyone as if they could see right through me and knew what I've been through. But, all they could see was the act I put on and the mask I wore to hide it. One thing I hated throughout my life is that I could fix everyone else's problems, but my life was considered a blob that sat in the dark. The sad thing is that the only way for me to see the light, was to open up and say the only thing I didn't want to say and face. The one nightmare that would replay and never end.

You may wonder why it took so long to open my mouth, like all I had to do was speak and it would all go away. Truth is... it's way easier said than done. I thought that if I said something, my past would be resurfaced, and I would have to re-live it all over again, which was something God knows I didn't want to happen. Telling and opening up about something bad happening to you is like knowing how to swim but not surviving a flood. You think you will make it until you crash and have no more fight left. But I had to say something, five years later, even if it meant I had to crash. I couldn't bear the pain anymore. I couldn't walk around in fear. I had to stand up and place my fallen crown on my head.

I am realizing my worth and who I am. I am a

Queen. I am a survivor. I am a warrior. I am a living testimony. The only way to survive and branch out was to open my mouth and speak out. The hardest part was to forgive. How do you even think about forgiveness when dealing with a demon?

When I opened up, it made me realize I wasn't alone in this. It also let me know who was on my side and who wasn't. I had to get rid of the negativity even if it meant losing my own blood. Once I spoke out, I thought, "Okay we got him, we did it!! He's going to jail." But, no. The part no one mentions that happens is being called a liar because I waited so long to speak.

No one warned me about having threats sent to me, people telling me that I wasn't going to make it in life, living in hiding, going to therapy, speaking with detectives, and random people popping up when I didn't want them to. Amazingly, none of that broke me. Trust me, it hurt a little...okay, it hurt like a thousand needles, but I got past it.

The one thing that did break me was telling my father, my blood, my protector, my king... What was his reaction? He didn't care. He never asked if I was okay or said he was on the way to where Paul lived, not any of that! When my father showed me that he didn't care and downplayed the situation, I just knew that meant I was worthless. At that point, I wanted to end it all.

Live? Why? For What? Why am I fighting?

Then I remembered all the victims that faced this before me, being molested by men and women close to them, and living their whole life afraid to speak. Some took it to their graves. I had to remind myself that I was still alive. I wasn't killed and didn't take my life to destroy my pain like other kids my age. If these poor harmless kids couldn't speak, I knew I had to. I must remember I am their voice, and I'm an example of them and who they are, even my siblings. I am the flame that never gets blown out. I am a child sexual assault survivor. I need all the parents and guardians to know this!! Never stop asking your child questions, never give up on them, and always fight for them. Never allow them to think they are not equal to you when deserving of respect.

To the kids that have faced this, even adults, open your mouth. You may be afraid, but just know you're saving others that could be going through the same ordeal now. Girls, never let your crown fall because we are all queens that run our palace with grace and dignity, and we need no jokers around to tell us otherwise. Guys, never let your flame burn out. Make sure that you are always burning with the passion to never give up. You (We) all are warriors.

Psalms 37:5 (ERV) - "Depend on the lord, trust him and he will help you."

Joshua 1:9 (ERV) - "Remember, I commanded you to be strong and brave. Don't be afraid, because the Lord your God, will be with you wherever you go."

Just imagine the truths of others like this and the people deceiving you with a candid camera smile every day. Deep down, they are still dealing with issues.

CHAPTER SIX
Now Whattt?

Moving forward. After Paul was jailed for four months, they let him out on house arrest. He thought he was free and started violating his orders. Due to his actions, he had to go back to court, in which I was there every step of the way. At the hearing for violating, Paul showed up with his family and the assistant church pastor. For you church folks, this may go over your head, but it has to be said. Then again, this is my truth, so I can only be as real as possible. If it was me, I would find out why a person was in jail ahead of time before coming to support them in court, I would collect all the facts first.

CHAPTER SEVEN

Stand Up For Something

~ DON'T FALL FOR ANYTHING ~

When you are considered a leading figure in the church, please have all the proper facts before supporting people whom you don't know. I don't care how well you think you may know that church member. Please don't get up and represent that person in court like they're an angel sent down from heaven. You don't have a clue of the number of kids and adults that this creep has molested.

Prime Example: When someone in the church passes away, you fight to send that deceased person to heaven and don't even know whether they loved or knew God. They could have been a person who didn't believe in God at all. Only the highest power is the one that can judge.

I suggest getting all the facts before standing behind the person you clearly don't know everything about. Don't be so sure as to what a person wouldn't do or what they have done. Because trust and believe, there is a chance you will be betrayed, and your beliefs will come back to bite you in the end.

CHAPTER EIGHT
Confessions

Back to the hearings - This man complained about needing to be home because of his bad health. Excuse me? Your bad health? What about my children's mental health, as well as the other kids? What about me wanting to kill a man for taking advantage of kids? He didn't think about any of that when he was out here messing with these kids for years. The jail has physicians and nurses; no empathy would be given over here, and I'm saying that as nicely as possible.

During this whole ordeal, I got a call from the prosecutor's office, saying they had some information to discuss with me. I couldn't even remember what was going on when they called. But I immediately got on the road and headed to the prosecutor's office to see what was so important. When I arrived, he sat me down in a room and explained to me that a now forty-year-old male had contacted them and said that he was ready to talk about what the accused Paul had done to violate him when he was younger. After learning of the accused being arrested, he felt it was time for him to come forth and confess. Can you imagine all these years holding this in, then one day you hear that the person you knew that took a part of you was finally in jail? You could get some relief to finally tell your truth.

Then, we came to a roadblock, and the system failed us once again. Due to his allegations taking place in another jurisdiction, the victim would have to go to that county to file a report on the accused, which would start another process. Then, on top of that, low and behold, there is a police report from the previous year for another little girl and her brother against Paul and his sister (the babysitter). However, the parents decided to just move out of the state and not press charges. Bull Crap –Not me!!

Coming back to a state of mind, I was suffering through these months with all kinds of negative thoughts in my head. I started the process of elimination, going back to individuals I could remember who were around my kids from the beginning of being babysat to whoever came in contact with them. I remembered the two girls that Delilah named. I tried to locate them, but came up empty. I continued my search for another individual who came to mind.

I made contact with Darlene, who was a relative of Paul. I instantly jumped for joy. It was strange that I was able to make that connection. But, I said if it was meant to be, it would happen, and it did. I got in contact with the young lady and arranged to meet with her, which took place at her home. I was lucky to have my friend, Nell, with me for moral support and also as a listening ear. At the end of the emotional meeting, Nell became everybody's support.

Darlene wanted to know more and bombarded us with questions about why I wanted to meet with her. Before we got into the details, I asked her why she stopped coming around the babysitter's house. Let me pause for a moment and go back. As I said, my mind was always in detective mode. I thought back to six months prior.

One day, while I was at work, Paul's sister (the babysitter) came by the job because she had an appointment and decided to say hello, as usual. But this time, in particular, she expressed that Darlene stopped letting her babysit her kids. What? Why? She proceeded to say that Darlene accused her brother, Paul, of touching her daughter. Go Figure.

CHAPTER NINE

The Reddest of All Red Flags

That was a red flag, but it didn't come back to my remembrance until I was sitting in Darlene's kitchen that evening. The Most High allowed me to know this six months prior to discovering what I would learn about my children's truth. Did I know all of this would make sense in the months to come? No, I didn't. God was just aligning the pieces together.

Darlene explained to me, right in front of her husband, how one night she was bathing her daughter Lalah, who was five at the time, and expressed how Lalah didn't want her to touch or wash her private area. Darlene asked her what was wrong. Lalah feared to tell her, thinking that she would get in trouble. Darlene pleaded with her to tell her what was wrong. Lalah finally broke down and said Paul had been touching her and began to point frantically at her private parts and say down there. Then, Darlene explained another incident where Paul took her and the kids to the store. She left the kids in the car while she went inside. When she returned, the accused was sitting in the back of the van with her daughter, Lalah.

He immediately got out of the van, and Darlene noticed him zipping up his pants. She was shocked and confused, trying to rationalize what was happening and what had taken place. The worst thoughts exploding through her mind couldn't possibly be a reality. Sorry, but if it was me, and I noticed something was not right, especially when dealing with my kids, I would have asked what was going on. Nobody would be moving out of that parking lot until I got some answers.

As parents, so many times, we see things but don't say anything. We don't want to believe the worst in people or feel like failures because we let something happen under our watch. Not me. Not ever again. I'll ask every question in the book and demand answers fast. Darlene chose to cut herself off from the family instead of going to the police and reporting this creep due to the shame and insecurity she felt. I explained to her what took place with my kids, and she was in total shock. I advised her to report him immediately for the sake of her daughter

Lalah's well-being and for so many others.

This truth is shared with many people, but they may not have as much strength to endure the exposure that takes place when confessing the truth. Many victims decide to keep quiet and keep the secrets to themselves out of fear, shame, and many other negative emotions. This should not be the case because, in the end, we're teaching our kids to stay quiet when there's trouble and not to say anything for as long as they can keep a secret. That is definitely not the way to be!

I battled hard with myself, asking if there was a way that I could have prevented this from happening altogether. The demons of the past sucked me in, and I pondered many 'what-ifs'. I rationalized that to remain in the present and help my kids as well as myself heal, sharing their story was the sacrifice that had to be made to spread the word about that evil demon, Paul (and so many other Pauls and Janes), as to what he'd done to my kids and many others for years.

I felt like I was running the investigation on my own. When I went to the police with leads, they would take their sweet time. If it was their child, they would have wasted no time making a move. I went as far as taking the recorded conversation with Darlene to the detectives, and they advised me that if she didn't press charges, they wouldn't be able to use the recording as evidence.

In moments like that, I feel like our judicial system keeps failing us. You're telling me I can have all the information about a crime, and still nothing happens? Shameful! I had so much evidence against this demon. Yet, it was all worthless. It was a slap in the face, but that small setback wasn't going to force me to give up! I was determined to be around to see justice served, no matter what it took and at what cost.

Trust Me, He Hasn't Forgotten

By this time, we had moved out of state. I traveled back and forth to make all court appearances. After a year and five months passed since the case began, the prosecutor called to tell me about the plea deal for the accused. With this in place, my kids wouldn't have to testify in court, which was the least of my worries. When you're telling the truth, you never waiver from what has to be said. The First 48, C.S.I., and my criminal justice classes were being put to good use.

One day, Angel came up to me crying, "Why do people keep asking why it took so long for me to come forward?" Before I replied, I thought about everything happening in America with the *Me Too* movement. I don't care whether it was 10, 20, 30, 40, or 50 years ago. When

and if a person is ready to talk about the pain they've suf-
fered, the timeframe shouldn't matter.

Word of Advice: If you know someone dealing with this type of situation or something similar, just be there for them, support their truth, and stand by their side. No one wants to be alone during times like that. They shouldn't be alone.

CHAPTER ELEVEN

Plea Deal...
~ DON'T FALL FOR ANYTHING ~

Now, getting back to the plea deal. The accused pleaded guilty and was sentenced to five years of probation. Yes, I said five years of probation!!! And he had to register as a sex offender. What else happened, you might ask? Nothing. That's it, no prison time! A bunch of B.S.!!! Nothing more or less. Do I feel justice was served? Nope. That is far from what I wanted to see happen to him. I wanted him to feel pain, sleepless nights, and so much more. Knowing the horrors my kids went through, this did not sit right with me. I wouldn't wish this ordeal on anyone, whether they're known to me or not.

The weak don't survive in this world. You have to stay consistent and strong throughout the entire process.

Find your strength within yourself, but don't let your resolve diminish. Seeing the expressions on my kids' faces when they heard the accused finally confess to his wrongdoing was priceless. They received the validation they were looking for that someone believed them and didn't give up fighting for them. I sure as hell didn't give up, especially when I felt like I'd failed them already. That portion of my truth is over.

When I attended the prayer retreat, the woman of God gave everyone instructions to take the little palm-sized wooden caskets and write little notes inside to be buried and never open again. Well, I decided to take two of them back home for my children, not knowing what would be buried. But, it was for a time such as this, the time after the case concerning them.

We took a trip to the beach, where I allowed them to write what they felt and put them in the little wooden caskets. Once the task was accomplished, the little wooden caskets met with the waves and began to float in the ocean. All the hurt and pain drifted away to no return. You can't keep holding on to dead things and situations. They need a proper burial, too. I have forgiven myself by being an advocate on behalf of my children, as well as others who have been sexually assaulted.

During this process, I chose to relocate them, which offered a rewarding new start and environment. I am truly grateful for that special friend who gave me the push to venture out into unknown territory in a quest for greater. Thank You K.P.

CHAPTER TWELVE

Reverse Needed to Escalate

Four months before I learned about my kid's ordeal, I finalized my divorce. Like, what a year. I started to question the Most High. What did I do to deserve such a horrible year? I was married four and a half years to whom I thought was the man of my dreams. I don't mean to speak ill of him. God knows I'm not perfect either, and I've done wrong and admitted my faults. However, I can own up to the mistakes that I've made.

When I was first introduced to my now ex-husband, we hit it off well. I didn't realize then that I was the type of person who needed to be in control and act like everyone's Momma, Nurturer. I was also an introvert. So, when I wanted you around, it was good, and when I wanted to be alone, people let me be (no harm intend-

35

ed). At the beginning of our relationship, those aspects never seemed to be an issue. Then, I started noticing the red flags.

CHAPTER THIRTEEN

Red Flags - Bloody Flags

Ladies, listen closely! Never... I repeat... Never ignore the red flags. They are red for a reason. Understand the danger. Even though I had my insecurities, my woman's intuition never led me astray. When a man starts staying out or working too late, and you find out they had a day off or was somewhere he didn't have any business, BE-WARE! Something isn't right!

Early one morning, the Most High woke me out of my sleep, and I started praying. Then, I opened up the Bible and started reading scriptures until I eventually fell back to sleep. You'll see this making sense soon. So, about five in the morning, my husband came into the house and said, "Get up; we need to talk!" "I'm up," I said sternly. Then, he proceeded to say Kara was pregnant, and my response was, "OKAY!?" The reasoning for my response is the fact that this chick is supposed to be his cousin, so I'm wondering why we are even talking about her this time of the morning.

Well, here's the kicker. Are you ready? Because I sure as hell wasn't! Here it comes! My husband bursts out and says, "She's pregnant with my baby." Hold up. Rewind it. Excuse me? Your baby? Dude, am I being punked right now?

It took a minute to process all of this, my head spinning and my face paler than ever. God sure does have a funny sense of humor. This is the reason why He had me up at three in the morning, praying and reading the Word. He was preparing me for what was about to take place. I truly felt in my heart that if I wasn't prepared for what my husband was telling me, there was going to be trouble, trouble, trouble (in my Bernie Mac Voice).

I asked my questions as well as gave my choice words. Then he started packing his belongings because he said he was leaving. I stopped him and said, "Stop, don't pack anything. We're going to get through this." Truth be told, that wasn't me saying that. It was the Most High in me, because my flesh wanted to make him feel what I felt, hurt and betrayed. By being so calm, he got scared. Let's just say he was more comfortable sleeping on the floor that night. I wasn't going to lay a hand on him, even though that little voice kept telling me to do some evil things to him and her. But, again, I found comfort in the word.

I called my mother, explaining to her what had taken place, and would you believe she stopped me in the middle of my rant and said, "Did Hillary leave Bill? Did Jessie Jackson's wife leave him? Then, if they didn't, who are you? Don't be so fast to leave. Did he lay a hand on you?" I said, "No, Ma'am." She then said, "You all can get through this."

Hear me good. This is coming from a woman who has never been married. Nevertheless, she knew the truth, which I didn't want to hear, but it was for my good. Even though I was hurting inside, I still got up and went to church that day. It didn't dawn on me what the reality of the situation was until the church service was over, and I had a major meltdown. I could hardly breathe, and my body convulsed like my brain was in overdrive. To think I have always been strong for everyone, but who was there for me when I was hurting?

Thank God for my church friend, Nell, who was there. Nell didn't ask questions but just held me, and that's what I needed. You should always have that person in your life who won't ask a million questions but just be there to listen when needed.

CHAPTER FOURTEEN

The Encounter

~ THE OTHER WOMAN ~

A few days later, I made contact with Kara and arranged for her, my husband, and I to talk face-to-face. When the day finally came, Baby, when I tell you I went to this meeting stepping like a boss. Trust me, I did. You are never supposed to look like what you're going through. I was dressed to the "T" to express my power over her, Satan, and the situation.

Before the meeting, I was quiet that whole day at work because I didn't know what I would face. But, I had to have my mind prepared and my heart cleared. My husband was so nervous when we finally met that evening, but I kept it together. Her mother and a family friend accompanied her to this meeting. I asked her with a calm voice what her intentions were and where we were supposed to go from here. In spite of the situation, the baby didn't ask to be conceived. I firmly believe that everything happens for a reason.

I graciously allowed her to speak. She told me everything. The number of times they had sex and that she was pregnant from him before, but she lost it. She admitted being upset on our wedding day because she wanted to be the one marrying him. Did I fail to mention this chick, Kara,, was at our wedding, helping us celebrate like everything was all good? If I had known that, I would have called it off, and she would have had her wish. I can't get over the fact that I was tricked into believing they were cousins. Boy, was I blind!

I remained calm throughout the meeting because KARMA is mighty sweet. When it was my turn to speak, I didn't sugarcoat a thing. Her mom was there, but if you're the type to mess with a married man, you shouldn't be hiding behind anyone. She pursued him even when she knew the dark results of her actions. I asked if she knew for sure that the child was his, and she said yes.

I declared that every moment until the baby was born also concerned me. Going to the doctor? I'll be there. Need to ask my husband something? I'll be listening to that conversation. This was the hand she dealt herself. And, my husband wasn't going to give her a dime, not until the DNA solidified the answers. Ladies, if more than one person is involved, please be honest. It's hurtful when the truth comes out. I told her I would oversee every crossed T and dotted I on any check written concerning the baby.

The meeting was finally over, and I felt disturbed. This type of situation happens around the world more than you can imagine. A majority of men/women desire a committed woman/man with desires of another one on the side. What's the point of cheating? Why bother to be in a relationship if you're not ready to be serious? Let people be!!!! Before you end up hurt or six feet under...

CHAPTER FIFTEEN

Then Comes Baby

Six months later, my husband got the call that the child was born. I couldn't show it, but I was in deep pain. Even though I had children prior to our marriage, and he assisted in raising them like they were his, it just wasn't the same being a wife who was not bearing his seed.

We proceeded to get dressed. I called my boss and told him I needed the day off. When I told my husband that I was accompanying him to the hospital, the look on his face was that of a child begging his parents not to embarrass him. I got the camera because a sister got to get pictures. Walking into the hospital room, Kara looked like she saw a ghost, stunned that we came together. Damn right, we came together. I hated his choices, but I decided to stand by him.

As all three of us walked to the nursery, I felt like I was walking the Green Mile. It was a dreaded walk, long and miserable. But I endured. My husband and Kara went in, and I stood by the window, taking my pictures. As angry as I was at the adults who betrayed me, I knew that baby was innocent and pure, a cutie pie, to say the least.

After visiting the nursery for a while, we proceeded back to the room. By then, the doctor was walking into the room and congratulated Kara on a great delivery. The doctor turned to my husband and asked if he was the father. He nodded, and I wanted to scream that they were wrong, hoping this was all a dream. When he looked at me and asked if I was the proud auntie, I wanted to scream louder. Instead, I remained the reasonable, level-headed one and kindly told the doctor that I was his wife. The doctor's face turned red, and he excused himself. He must have been wondering what in the Hell was going on. It was a really awkward moment, and the tension in the air increased tremendously.

On the way from the hospital, we experienced the quietest ride back home. I had to bite my tongue to keep from crying, screaming, shouting, and breaking things. I mustered up every iota of strength in my body to keep a cool head and not overreact. When we arrived home, I was mentally drained from the chain of events that day.

I took a nap, and he came and laid next to me. I didn't have the energy to say no to him or push him away. He was my husband, after all.

The phone rang, breaking my moment of peace. It was Kara, crying because her baby girl couldn't be released from the hospital without registering her last name. I advised her to refer back to our meeting six months prior, where I stated that nothing would be done until paternity was established. Nothing had happened yet, so, therefore, I told Kara to give that baby her last name so they could go home. My husband's name could be attached once the proof of DNA was established.

My detective instincts kicked in, and I asked myself why she was trying so hard to put my husband's name on the birth certificate without following my advice first. Still, I helped him fill out the child support papers, which took two months to get a court date. I wasn't in a hurry to finalize anything. When the court date came, we showed up, but she didn't (RED FLAG). They swabbed his mouth in case she brought the baby at a later time to have it done.

We set up another court date, and guess what? No show again! I was frustrated at her for wasting everyone's time playing these games. If the child was his, all she had to do was prove it. Then we could continue our lives and be a part of this child's upbringing. This side chick of his was making my life a living hell for the last seven months. Trust me, never once did I put all the blame on her because it takes dos (two). My husband and I were having little hiccups even before I found out about Kara as being more than a kissing cousin. And, Lord knows that wasn't easy, but I hung in there.

CHAPTER SIXTEEN

The Kicker

Before we knew it, the child was five months old. We received a call from child support stating that no further tests were needed. Another dude – yes, add another man to the mix – had tested ninety-nine point ninety-nine percent as the baby's father. Now, I'll be James Brown. The crazy thing is that my husband was hurt. He probably is still hurting to this day. Why? Did he really want that baby girl to be his? I don't truly know what was going through his mind. But I'll be damned if I waste my time trying to figure it out.

There was one thing I couldn't stop thinking about. That Heffa knew all along that the baby belonged to someone else and didn't say a word.

The question remained: where do we go from here?

I was relieved that he never signed the birth certificate. As you can guess, I wasn't fond of the situation, but I was prepared to assist in raising that baby girl as one of my children. She didn't deserve to suffer because of an adult's mistake. Still, I felt like we dodged a bullet, and there was a glimmer of hope that my husband and I could rebuild again.

I naïvely thought everything was going well. Whenever you've been betrayed, it seems like you never fully trust the betrayer again. You may tolerate them but not fully trust them. Never let your guard down or stop praying. Continue to seek the Most High for guidance.

A few months went by, and my intuition kicked in again. Ladies/Men, we must be aware of the people we attract because before you know it, you will start sabotaging any relationship as you'll be drawn to the same type of mate but with a different name.

I was heartbroken when I discovered my husband and his female coworker were having an affair. I confronted her with a fire in my belly, and she acted like they were just good friends. (Like Biz Markie, "But you say, He's just a friend.") Then, she told me about things he had shared with her concerning our marriage.

Important Note to the Men and Women Out There:
1. Whatever is going on in your home, let it stay there.

2. Don't take your problems to people who have no business knowing about it.

3. If you need someone to vent to, talk to the Most High or speak with a counselor or someone close that will not judge but tell the truth.

4. But never the one you're creeping with because they will hold it over your head. A counselor or confidante knows how to listen. And though they will form their own opinions, they will allow you to decide the right thing to do without swaying your opinion.

Learn the value of privacy because if you and your significant other decide to reconcile, then that will be between you two and not the entire world. Learn from my experiences!

Like I said before, back in Chapter 12, I'm not going to sit up here and paint this picture like I was the perfect wife because I wasn't. Did I have flaws? Yes. There were times when my husband wanted a little love and affection, and I pushed him away. What people don't understand is that if you grew up in a household where affection toward the opposite sex was not displayed, then how are you supposed to really know how to show someone something you never saw? I would rather keep it real than be phony. Even though I wasn't the type to go out and party, the fact that I just worked and stayed home, I assumed I was doing alright. But I guess I did make an ASS out of myself for assuming. Always remember, a person will make time for what's important to them.

As I remember it, his female coworker was married. I told her that I would be contacting her husband about what was going on. I had evidence of text messages and photographs that I could send to him. Let's just say that little fling ended really quickly...

CHAPTER SEVENTEEN

Test Designed Testimony

A few months after that altercation, my husband fell ill. One day, I had just walked into the house after work when I received a call from the hospital. They said they were struggling to reach my husband. He didn't understand the severity of his condition and needed to return to the hospital immediately. My stomach twisted into knots when I asked what she meant. The nurse blurted out over the phone he had cancer and we needed to get to the hospital right away.

This news hit me like a truck: no warning or time to process the information, no time for emotions bubbling to the surface, and no energy to shout about him keeping secrets from me. I had to start the car and drive. I prayed with all my might that God's will be done. When

we arrived, they prepared him for tests and chemother-
apy. This was a serious matter. My concern and anger
swirled through me, smashing against each other in a
will to be the most prominent emotion.

I reminded the Lord that He helped me through all
of what I dealt with in the last year, and I know that He
will continue to watch over and get me through this. I
truly thank the Most High for my spiritual father and
pastor, along with a handful of other strong people in my
life who rallied around and prayed around the clock for
him. It was an up-and-down battle, but by the strength
of God, we made it. I know God had a plan for his life as
well as mine.

CHAPTER EIGHTEEN
Better Than Better

Fast forwarding through the months, everything was better again, and my husband was in remission. Unfortunately, Satan took hold of my husband, and he started drinking and partying. That was the last straw. My anger consumed me, and I felt alone in the relationship and empty. I thought God wanted me around to help him through the ordeals. I started questioning my purpose as a wife. I prayed and found reassurance in the fact that I had done more than what others would have done. I thanked God for my patience and strength to keep moving forward. I had to realize I couldn't save him because I wasn't GOD.

CHAPTER NINETEEN
Facing Reality

Sadly, we have reached the point in the relationship where it came down to... the divorce. There were many bitter moments throughout the process. But, now we can laugh and talk like nothing ever happened.

Thinking back to my wedding day, as plain as day, I heard a voice speaking to me loud and clear that this man wasn't meant to be my husband. At the time, I thought it was just wedding jitters. (Even though my spiritual mom already warned me.) What could I do about it? All of our family, friends, and spectators were in this church to celebrate with us. I couldn't run out on a whim and disappoint them. I was committed and couldn't stop now. Besides, the wedding bill was paid in full.

Sometimes, I felt like I was being punished for rushing to find a partner to lay with and for the convenience of playing house with someone I thought would provide for me and my family, only keeping it real. I didn't wait for the man the Most High was sculpting for me.

We've all made choices that we have and will regret. No one is an exception. I just didn't want to keep shacking, as the old people would say. I knew I brought some of these issues on myself, and I must live with that, like trying to be hard at times and not showing affection, among other things that could drive a man out in the streets.

CHAPTER TWENTY

Give Us This Day
~ WELL, NEVERMIND ~

Coming to the present time, after the divorce and the court case with the children, we're bringing everything to a head. My family was searching for some sense of normalcy despite the chaos. Still, I must reveal one last piece of my life that I openly share to bring you wisdom.

Two years ago, I filed for child support for two of my kids against the father they always knew. It was not done out of being a bitter mom because that wasn't me. It took place to allow him to know that he would have to do his part once and for all. We went to court on Valentine's Day. Not exactly a day of love for us. After all these years, the father claimed that he knew my daughter was his but was unsure about my son. There was talk about that back in the day, but...

One night, I was having a good time with friends and ran into a dude I knew in middle school. I'll admit that we hooked up. That was the first and last time. It is true what they say; it only takes one time. I was only dealing with one other man at the time: my kids' father.

Okay, back to the court day. I went to my mom's house to get my son for the paternity test. After a few long weeks of waiting, the DNA results came back and said that his father wasn't the biological father he knew. I hid the results in my purse for a few weeks, not knowing how to share the news with my son. I prayed for God's guidance on the next steps of my life.

I decided to contact the only other dude who could be the father. The man from that night fourteen and half years ago. I found him on social media and reached out to him. He didn't respond until a month later. This was the first time we'd talked in over fourteen years! He said he knew I was pregnant with his child the whole time. Why wouldn't he ever say anything? He told me he never brought it up because I didn't pay attention to him when he tried to ask. I honestly couldn't remember everything that happened those years ago. I was intoxicated, truth be told.

I'm going to be truthful with mine. I knew I had to break the information to my son soon. Due to wanting to know the truth, I paid for DNA to be established, and we had the paternity test performed together. The results came on the weekend of Father's Day (how ironic). The crazy thing was my son's biological dad and I had been conversing on the phone since we made contact. My son kept asking to meet the dude that I'd been talking to lately on the phone. He didn't have a clue how drastically his life was about to change. Well, at least I thought...

CHAPTER TWENTY-ONE
Momma's Baby
~ DADDY'S MAYBE.. ~

The weekend came that I made the decision to tell my son the truth. He and I were on the road driving back home from out of town. My heart pounded as I thought about what I would say. Panic rose through my body.

Out of nowhere, I broke down and told him everything. I was shocked when he handled it so well. He commented on him and his sister not looking alike. I told him that all my children looked like me, and that's what mattered. We were able to laugh about it, bringing some relief.

That evening, I took my son to meet his biological dad at his job. It was one of those priceless moments that you want to cherish forever. My body had been cleansed of all the secrets, and my truth was out. This is me.

I was thrilled when they started building a relation-ship, and my son got the opportunity to meet a whole other family that welcomed him in as if they knew him forever. I am very grateful. But, then, the dad decided to move away. I could tell my son was devastated, which tore me apart. He never said what or how he felt except that he didn't really know him anyway. The fact that he gained more siblings, another grandmother, and a family made it all worth it.

The great thing that came from this situation is that the father he originally knew all his life never left his side. They actually formed a better, stronger relation-ship than ever before. God never ceases to amaze me. He gave me the strength to ask for forgiveness from those that I needed it from who were involved in the situation. After all those years, it was necessary; I had to make it right.

CHAPTER TWENTY-TWO
Forgive & Release

Angel

My past is my past, and it is something that I only choose to talk about when I feel that I am ready, which is now. My past is something that happens to many children. However, dealing with it is always handled differently.

I've learned to cope with my past by being involved in my community with several organizations and staying busy. I also listen to music. I love helping other girls on campus who have experienced similar situations in their lives like me.

Through the process of forgiveness, which is not fully there, I am trying every day to forgive the demon who attempted to take everything from me. I do forgive my mother, because I understand that it wasn't her fault as to what took place. She never knew. But when she did find out, she put in the work to see that justice was served.

Dexter

Some things happened in my past that I vowed never to talk about, but I found a way to cope with the pain of what took place and what it put me through. Weed was my way out of everything that I went through. I know people have plenty of opinions, but truth be told, it stopped me from taking my life so many times. What happened to me messed my head up mentally. Yeah, I may put a smile on my face, but deep down inside, I was hurting.

It was real pain behind rolling a blunt. Between what happened to me when I was younger to finding out the dad that I knew all my life wasn't my real dad, really hurt. But I'm making it. I just wish my real dad wouldn't have entered my life if he had intentions to leave again. I forgive my mother for her not knowing what took place with me. She didn't know, and my sister and I kept it to ourselves. She works her butt off to put clothes on our backs and food on the table. I love her, and it ain't her fault. Mom, I forgive you.

Delilah

Dealing with my past, to be honest, is the furthest thing in the back of my mind, or at least I try to keep what happened back there. I can say what took place has made me form a nonchalant attitude. There isn't anything that anyone can say or do that could break me down any further than what took place. My music is my outlet. I'm not going to lie, I tried to smoke to see if it would take away the pain. But, it didn't. So, I did not continue doing that.

Forgiveness for me is something I do often, even when it's not deserved. I don't like to hate. I don't blame anyone for anything anymore. It is what it is. I find it stupid that pedophiles can almost get away with the things they do to children, but people who steal and blue-collared criminals get harder sentences. I could never forgive Paul for what he did to me and my siblings and all the other children. I truly believe his sister knew what was happening. This is something that they are gonna have to live with...

CHAPTER TWENTY-THREE

What Can I Surrender

I surrender my time, joy, love, and happiness to make sure that everyone who comes in contact with me leaves fulfilled or at least has a will to thrive and live. As you have read or listened to my truth, I leave no corner untouched. This is the rawness, realness, the truth.

So many times, I put tasks before the most important people. I wanted them to know the value of working and that nothing was just going to be handed to them on a silver platter. However, yet, I failed, and I admit it. No more. I have begun to take time out for my tre, myself. I've learned to say "NO" and sometimes disconnect from everything altogether to keep my peace, and it's working for me. So, therefore, maybe you need to try it. My Tre (self), I spread advocacy for the children and adults who are afraid to speak up against sexual assault matter. For the men and women that have been going through relationship issues, you all matter. My family, friends, and associates matter!!!!!

CHAPTER TWENTY-FOUR
My Truth Pointers 360.. 240.. 180

Here are a few pointers for living life. Loyalty is key in any relationship. Sometimes, you don't always have to get the last word in. Shut the ... up. Pause, reflect, and get focused. Take time to meditate. Learn some breathing techniques. Before your feet hit the ground in the morning, have a talk with the Most High. Put the Phone Down! It's just a distraction at times.

Began to LOVE ON YOU before you can begin to love anyone else. Give yourself a minute to get it together. Go lay on somebody's couch (Therapist) and talk your issues out. Trust me, it helps. Never be afraid to fall. You can always get back up!!!

Now, I understand why I went through all of those hardships to reach this point in my life. If all of that was necessary to transform me into who I was meant to be today, then so be it. I've learned many lessons during my moments of truth.

By being single, I have been shaped into the woman I am proud to be. I can say that when my King finds me, or should I say when we meet, I will be prepared, willing, and able to be a loving Queen to him. Keep the Most High at the center of your relationship and watch it flourish.

Always remember to listen to the children; they are our future. Take time to nurture them, love on them, and, most importantly, support them. Never be so busy that a child lacks your attention. Before being their friend, you are the Parent/Guardian. You may not always agree with everything they may say or do, but hear them out. Never be afraid to discuss sex or the private parts with your children. You may be actually surprised by what they already know.

Please take action if a child ever confides in you concerning being sexually abused. And in that case, just give them a better understanding of what it is to be touched in the wrong way, along with the consequences. Follow your heart/intuition in all relationships, friendships, situationships, etc. They always tell the truth, even if it hurts.

Never be afraid to live! You only have one life to live. Make it Count!!!!!

Grateful Is Me

Much love and peace to those who took the time to hear my truth. It's taken me years to summon the courage to unveil my story, to let you into the deepest chambers of my soul. I hope you have found in my experiences and the reflection of my life a mirror of yours. Now that you've walked this path with me, I hope it touches a chord within you. My prayer is that you have learned something about yourself and how to handle the tests and challenges that the Most High hands to you. Only He can navigate you through them. Yet, in these trials, we discover an untapped well of strength we never knew we possessed. In every adversity, there's an opportunity for personal growth, transformation, and the reclamation of our power. Bring your power, not your pity.

It's not about asking, "Why me?" when life throws curveballs. Instead, it's about boldly proclaiming, "Why not me?" Each twist and turn in the journey, obstacle, and heartache were integral to our becoming. It had to happen. It was necessary. God said, "I'm putting you back to the place before the children were assaulted, before the court case and the divorce." He is restoring me to the place before the great fall. I will never go back to the beginning of 360 degrees, just 180, because going back is Not an Option.

In the echoes of The Divine, I heard the promise of restoration. A return to the place before the shadows fell, before the children were assaulted, before the courtroom battles and the fractures of a marriage. A return to a place of newfound strength and unwavering resolve. It's a transformation that doesn't loop back to the beginning but advances to a profound 180 degrees. For going back is truly "Not an Option."

In these words, I hope you find not just my story but a reflection of your journey. We are all on this path, encountering the unexpected and facing challenges that test the limits of our resilience. May my experiences serve as a beacon of hope and a testament to the strength in each of us. As we embrace our stories, our truths, and the inevitability of life's trials, we embrace our power.

Strength isn't a gift awarded to a select few; it is cultivated through the crucible of adversity. It doesn't come from consistently winning but from facing hardships head-on and deciding not to surrender. Arnold Schwarzenegger wisely said, "Strength does not come from winning. Your struggles develop your strengths. When you go through hardships and decide not to surrender, that is strength."

So, as you embark on your journey, remember the strength you've discovered within yourself and the power you hold to shape your destiny. The road ahead may be uncertain, but your newfound strength and unwavering spirit will guide you through the darkest nights and lead you to the dawn of a brighter day. Embrace it, for it is the essence of your truth.

My Daily Affirmations

The way to pray that assisted me in developing a prayer life:

A- adoration

C- confession

T- thanksgiving

S- supplication

Whatever you do, keep saying your Name. The more you say your name, the more it will be mentioned in places aligned with your now!!

- I am surrounded by abundance.

- I am wealthy.

- I am prosperous every day.

- I allow myself to breatheeee.

- I decree the plowman overtakes the reaper blessing. (Amos 9:13)

- I decree Psalm 66 as you come into your wealthy place.

- I decree strategic ideas come to you, as Isaiah 48:17 states.

- Continue to write the vision and make it plain. (Habbaukk 2:2)

- Nothing happens until something happens.

- My children are queens and kings. Uplift them and treat them as such.

Acknowledgment

To my Mom, without you, there would be no me. I am indeed forever grateful.

To my dad, thank you.

To R. Massey, thank you for sharing your passion for prayer with the world. Continue to transform lives through many more encounters and just being You!!

To the G's (my personal power couple), thank you for being there. Sometimes, just your presence was enough.

To MB, thank you for the push to get this of many more projects completed. (Habbakuk 2:2)

To my Tre, because of you all, I AM ENOUGH, I AM STRONGER, I AM WISER
 You all saved my life...

References

Brainyquote.com. (2024) Strengths Quotes. Retrieved from https://www.brainyquote.com/topics/strengths-quotes